A
RIGHT ROYAL
COLLECTION

A
RIGHT ROYAL
COLLECTION

PHOTOGRAPHS BY MIKE LLOYD

CAPTIONS BY JOHN LANGDON

with contributions from Gren and Arnold Wilson

COLUMBUS BOOKS

LONDON

Photographs copyright © 1985 Mike Lloyd

First published in Great Britain in 1985 by
C O L U M B U S   B O O K S
Devonshire House, 29 Elmfield Road, Bromley, Kent BR1 1LT

British Library Cataloguing in Publication Data

Lloyd, Mike
A right royal collection.
    1. Royal houses — Great Britain — Pictorial works
    2. Great Britain — Kings and rulers — Portraits
    I. Title
    941. 085'8'0922   DA28.1

ISBN 0-86287-236-7

Designed by Fred Price

Printed and bound by
R.J. Acford, Chichester, Sussex

In the course of duty, Mike Lloyd has spent fourteen years photographing the Royal Family. His collected works appear here for the first time in one volume, a monument both to his patience and to the forebearance of those who feature in the photographs. A recent portrait of Mr Lloyd in his working clothes is reproduced below.

All dressed up and nowhere to open...

'_Now_ they tell me I should be at the Trooping of the Colour!'

'My God – she's right!'

'There's just got...

'I like to see the reflection of my face on my boots.'   'I prefer to see the servant's.'

Bridesmaid Revisited?

...to be a loo...

'Why is there always a 21-gun salute when I've got a headache?'

'That's me and the wife in Ibiza...'

here somewhere.'

'Damn thing keeps slipping down.

...Never mind,

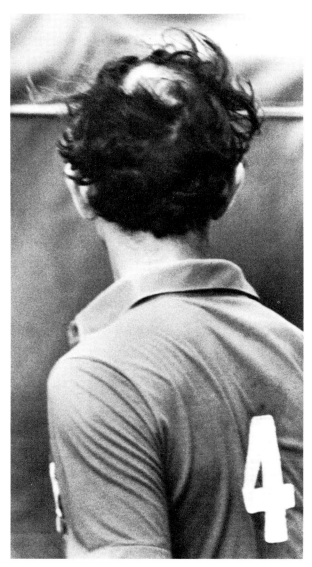

it'll never show... under a crown.'

'Net curtains make
such practical presents.'

'My God – isn't that Mother in the crowd?'

'Well, where was it when you last saw it?'

'If anyone else
asks me for a
hundredweight of
nutty slack, I'll
have Ian MacGregor
on to him.'

'... and tell that
Cartland woman the cucumber
face-pack was a disaster.'

'Oh, sod – its head's come off.'

'Course you could do it.'

'I suppose I'm about the right age, but...'

are you sure the Shadows are still auditioning?'

'Ach, ja, now I remember him – little moustache and hair down his forehead like zo...?'

'Toss over the new batteries – she's stopped again.'

'Use your hanky!'

'Charles! How many <u>more</u> times?!

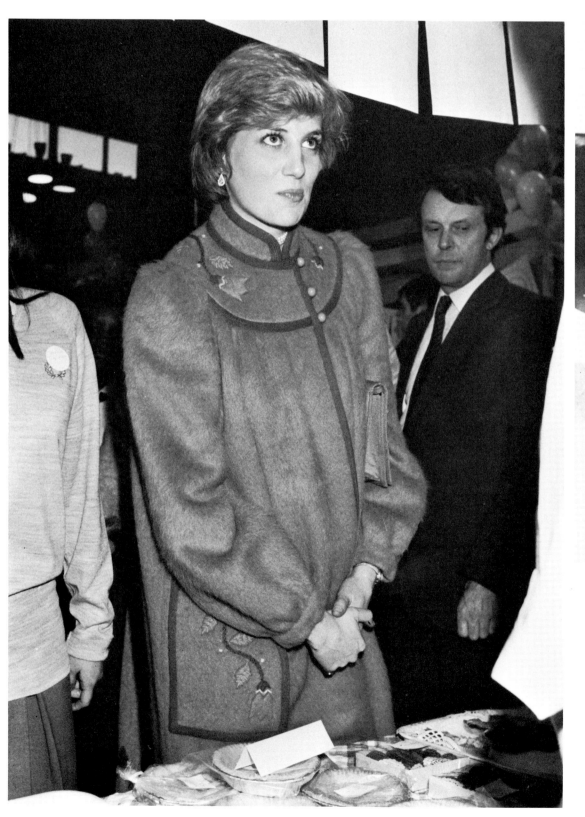

'Bat's eggs? How charming.'

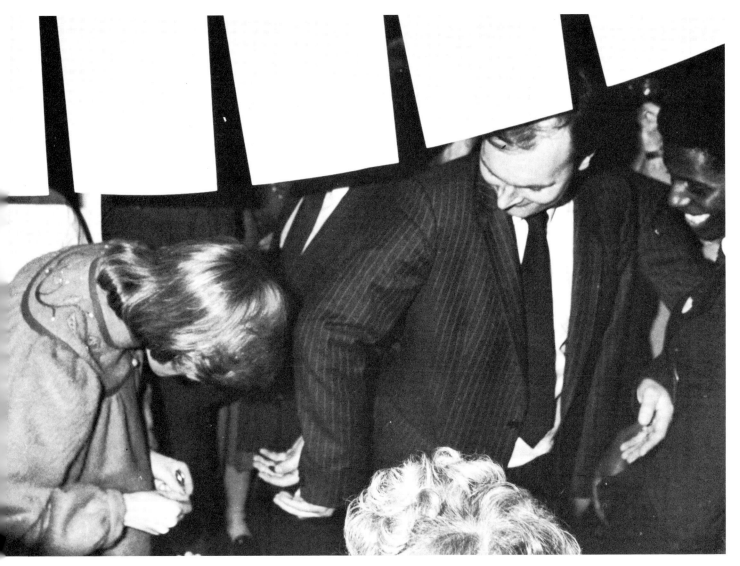

e never has enough loose change handy for tipping one's detectives.'

'You won't forget to
write, will you?'

'You can come out now,
Diana – the photographers
have gone.'

'Commander Bond here, Ma'am – Special Branch...'

'Charles — how do you get an Irish girl pregnant?'

'Er...

...I don't know...

you'll have to tell me.'

'And you thought the Irish were stupid!'

'I don't get it.'

'That's not what I've heard.'

'We'll never get back in time for <u>Dallas</u> now.'

'Damn! We've missed last orders.

Who makes these stupid laws?'

'Yes, I know, but you've got to give the marriage a chance, Mother — after all, it's only the second day.'

'No, no, Andrew – the Pope was last week.'

'No – that's your elbow: you sit on the other one.
Ronnie can't tell the difference either.'

'Charles Philip Arthur George...

...come on down!!'

'Thank God there weren't any photographers about.'

'It's o.k., Charles – they've found the horse.'

'Just keep calm and don't let the customs officer catch your eye.'

'My trouble is... my wife _does_ understand me.'

'I say, Mother — will you tell him or shall I?

'Don't look now, Anne darling, but your Shetland pony has gone.'

'Just once more, Anne,
and then you'll have to
practise by yourself.'

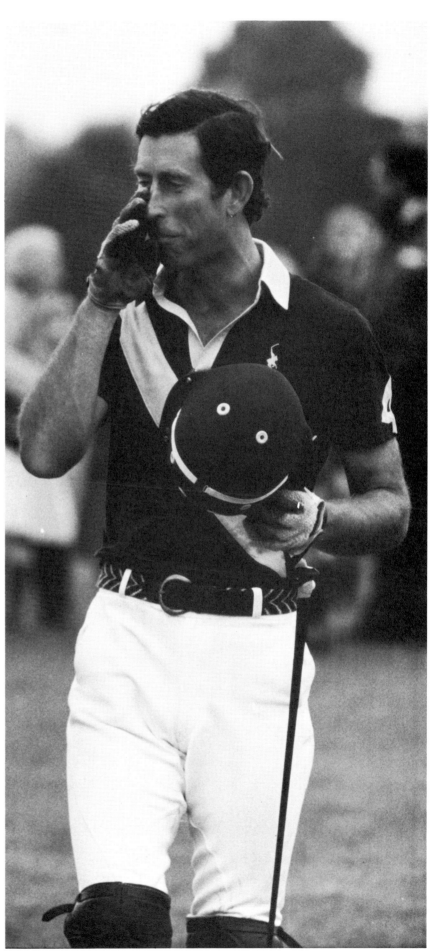

'I must see a man about a corgi –
know what I mean?...

...no more curried eggs for me.'

'Damn — I was hoping for the cuddly toy.'

'I hope he doesn't notice it's upside down.'

'He never does it if he sees you watching

'Bar-bar-bar, bar-Barbour Anne.'

'Foggy's so common – he just won't pay the admission price.'

'Oh my God – it's fallen off...

What the hell am I going to tell her this time?'

'Sorry, sir – it's not round here either.'

'What do you call that place we use for picnics?'   *'Gloucestershire, Sir.'*

'I'm sure I had it when I came...

...nope – at least I don't think it's mine...

'You mean <u>you</u> didn't attach the horse-box either?'

I remember putting it somewhere   Ah, there you are!   ... Now I can rest easy, knowing the
safe in case of barbed wire...   country's future is in safe hands.'

'Well, actually we've hired a nanny already.'

'Is there a back way
I could use, doctor?'

'For goodness' sake, Diana –

it really is time...

someone de-loused the corgis.'

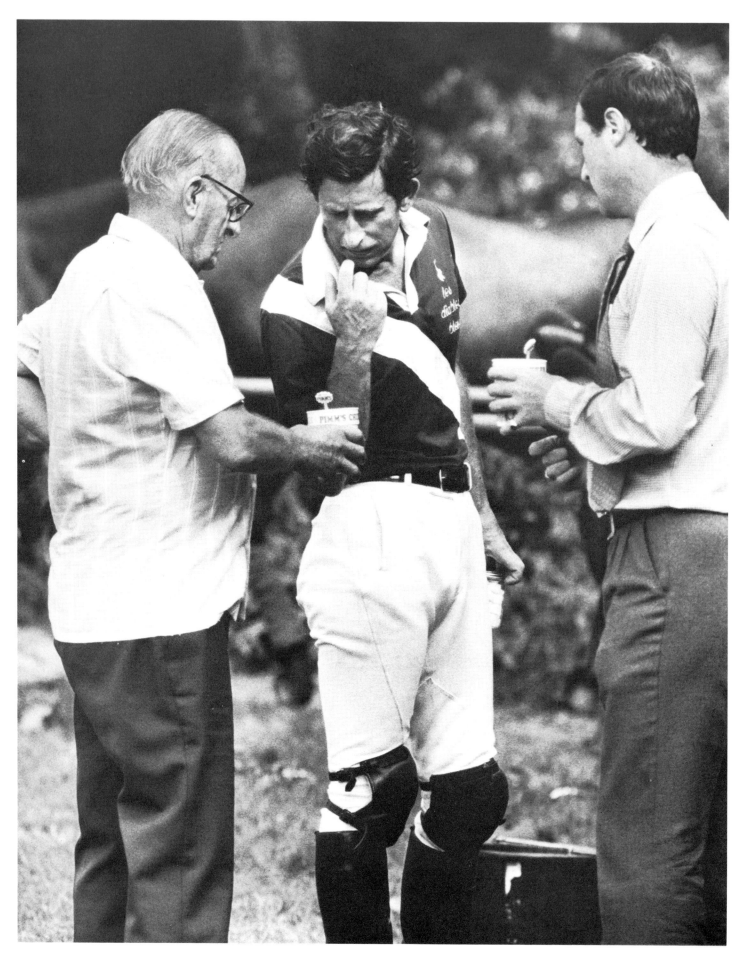

'Well, if they're <u>not</u> pot noodles...

Dad, have you lost any of your fishing things?'

Is it a bird...?

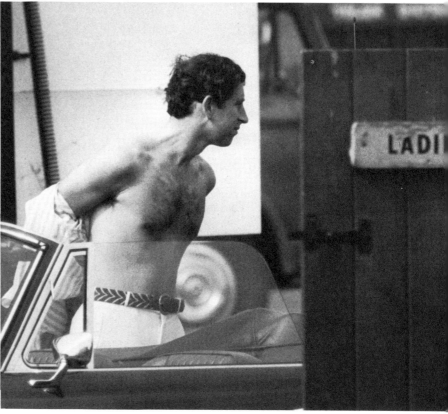

Is it a plane...?

No... it's Superklutz!

'Tell your brother he can keep his flowers... and leave *my friend* alone.'

'Did someone mention scoring?'

'Opened Parliament, trooped the colour, knighted old Thingy – no
doubt about it, I'm in a career rut.'

'How can I expect an all-over tan with this ruddy fringe?'

'Sorry, darling – can't seem to find your fruit gums anywhere.'

'Do try it on, Mummy –
Mrs Reagan would be so disappointed...'

'I declare this conversation open.'

'It'll stunt your growth.'

'I warned you...'

'Button your lip, smartarse – he's mine.'

'Your palace or mine?'

'Mum says there's a delivery for you from Harrods.'

'Congratulations!'

'It's a boy!'

'What do you mean,   they wouldn't give us accident insurance?'

'We've claimed on it twice already.'

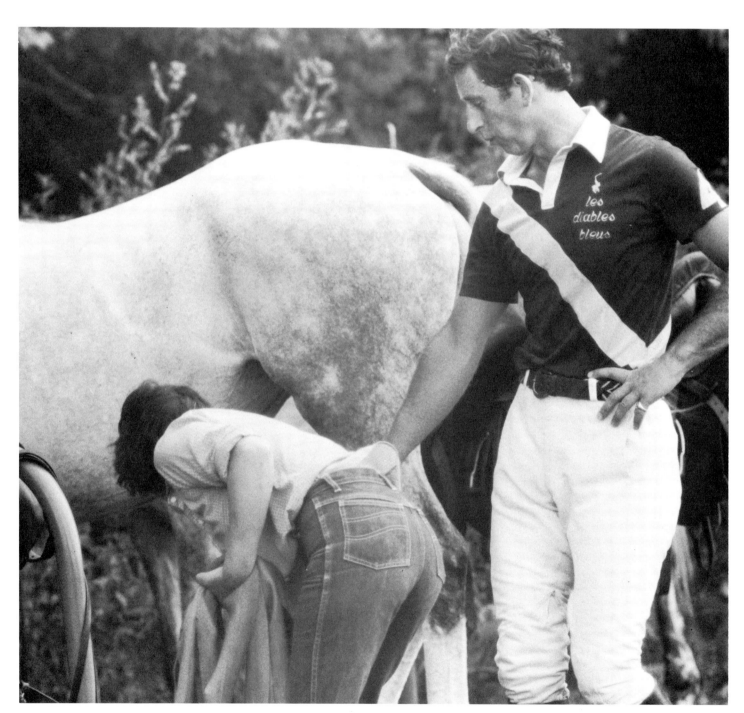

'If there are four, it's a cow.'

'Oh well –
if you're not
rgaret Rutherford
you can have the
autograph back.'

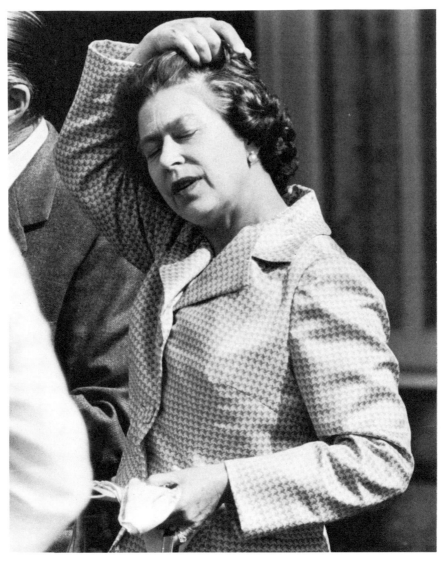

'Have they hidden the join, dear?'

*'I've told you, you're wasting your time with Edward VIII
impressions – she's never going to abdicate!'*

Send her victorious...

happy...   *...and glorious...*

Long to bloody rain over us...

God save me.

'I'll name that tune in one.'